The Thatched Houses of Cou

GW01091516

FOREWORD

In 1987, the Office of Public Works commissioned a survey of thatched cottages in County Kildare. A review of this survey was identified as an action in the County Kildare Heritage Plan (2005-2009) in order to assess the level of attrition of loss of thatched houses in the intervening years. Funding for the review was secured from Kildare County Council, the Heritage Council and the Department of the Environment, Heritage and Local Government, and has provided the basis for this publication.

Thatched houses are an important part of out national heritage and are often recognised as an integral part of our Irishness. They are, however, becoming an increasingly rare sight. The number of surviving cottages in Kildare has declined from 92 in 1987 to 55 in 2005. Most surviving thatched houses are of great significance to the cultural, historical and architectural identity of the county. They remain a tangible link with the past, offering the passer-by the opportunity to appreciate such unique features as undulating wall surfaces, small sash windows and oaten thatch with deep eaves overhanging the walls. The image evoked by their plank half doors is a distinctively Irish one.

Thatched houses should not, however, be viewed only in terms of the contribution they make to our interpretation of the traditions and customs of previous generations. They are essentially viable and practical places to live, and they are capable of responding to contemporary needs and living standards: many of the surviving houses are testimony to this.

This publication is intended to raise awareness of thatched cottages as a special element of Kildare's heritage and to prompt actions to protect the declining asset that they represent.

Niall Bradley
County Manager

INTRODUCTION

Kildare County Council commissioned Charles Duggan, Architectural Heritage Advisor with Stephen Farrell, to revise a thatch survey compiled during 1986-1987 by Michael Higginbotham of the Office of Public Works (OPW). The Higginbotham Survey identified 92 thatched buildings in Kildare, of which 55 survive with varying degrees of intactness. Two additional thatched cottages, previously unidentified, were also found. As a means of determining the future of the existing stock of thatched buildings and the thatch industry in the county, the revised survey aimed to assess the rate of attrition and loss, and identify the attitudes and perceptions to thatch. The revised survey took place between April and September 2005.

The National Inventory of Architectural Heritage (NIAH) format was used to build up a record of each structure, and to build upon the data compiled in the 1987 survey. Where possible, sketch floor plans of interiors have been carried out. In most cases, floor plans were prepared without access to interiors and were based on observations including the position of chimneystacks, the front door and window openings. Each standing habited structure was measured externally.

In addition to the revision of the 1987 survey, tin-roofed houses, which were excluded in the former survey, were identified. This addition cannot claim to be exhaustive, though it is unlikely that many more than the 55 tin-roofed houses identified will be found.

We are indebted to the owners and occupiers of these thatched buildings, who took the time to speak with the survey team and were so forthcoming with valuable historical and anecdotal information. We would like, in particular, to thank Jack Donohue (thatcher) and Eddie Molloy (son of Pat Molloy, thatcher) who were helpful in building a picture of the thatching tradition in the county.

Fig. 1: This house in Killeen West represents both the simplicity and grace that a well-maintained thatched house embodies.

"Rural vernacular or traditional architecture is the construction of small plain buildings in the countryside (particularly before 1925) where the dominant influence is siting, materials, form and design in the local folk tradition. Such vernacular buildings will have been typical of a common type in any given locality and will lack the individualism and educated design features that characterised international fashions in formal architecture during the same period. Rural vernacular houses may be recognised as such by meeting most of the primary characteristics listed..."
Historic Buildings Council, Townland Survey, 1996-97
in Northern Ireland

The thatched buildings of County Kildare are represented by quite distinct characteristics. Many of these relate to the materials used in their construction, alterations which have been made in the past, and the prevailing tastes for functional and decorative detailing, such as the twisted or roped ridge with bobbins to either end.

Prevailing Characteristics in County Kildare

Of the thatched houses surveyed in County Kildare, the following characteristics have been noted. In some cases a cottage surveyed may exhibit more than one characteristic.

- Windbreakers or shallow porch projections which are not partitioned internally and simply form a prolonged lobby.
- Lobby entrance to central bay (not formally placed to centre).
- Direct entry to kitchen with opening located at farthest end from the hearth.
- Porch extensions to both lobby and direct-entry houses.
- Oaten thatch with twisted or roped ridge with bobbins.
- Artificial slate/corrugated metal/slate roof covering to single-bay pitched roof extensions, mostly c. mid-twentieth century.

- Extensions placed at either end of the house, sometimes forming byres.

Characteristics of Irish Vernacular Architecture

- Absence of a formal floor plan.
- Absence of drawing or written specification.
- Presence of a linear, elongated rectangular plan.
- Typical depth of six metres.
- Mass load-bearing walls.
- Hearths and chimneys located along the axis of the linear plan.
- Door openings in long walls into kitchen.
- Doors and windows on long walls, and a linear house form which is extended along its length or by the addition of a second storey.[1]

---

1. Buttermer, N., Rynne, C., Guerin, H., (eds), *The Heritage of Ireland*. The Collins Press, Cork.

The values attributed to vernacular architecture, and our understanding of their significance, is greatly enhanced by such categorisations. While the characteristics are applicable countrywide, each county exhibits nuances that generally defy categorisation. The most obvious contrast in type is between the stone built, gabled thatched houses of the west of Ireland and the low slung, clay-walled, hipped roof houses of the eastern regions. These regional variations and local traditions are subtle evidence of the endurance of local practices and preferred methodologies which would have been handed down orally from generation to generation.

ICOMOS Charter on The Built Vernacular Heritage (Mexico, 1999)

The International Committee of Monuments and Sites (ICOMOS) has ratified a charter on built vernacular heritage. The charter recognises that vernacular heritage is "the fundamental expression of the culture of a community, of its relationship with its territory[...]". The charter identifies the issues currently facing this heritage as "problems of obsolescence, internal equilibrium and integration". These are the issues which currently face both the local authorities and owners of thatched houses alike. The charter sets down the principles of conservation with regard to the vernacular built heritage, and it is the challenge of both local authorities and owners of thatched buildings to address these principles.

Principles of Conservation

1. The conservation of the built vernacular heritage must be carried out by multidisciplinary expertise while recognizing the inevitability of change and development, and the need to respect the community's established cultural identity.

2. Contemporary work on vernacular buildings, groups and settlements should respect their cultural values and their traditional character.

3. The vernacular is seldom represented by single structures, and is best conserved by maintaining and preserving groups and settlements of a representative character, region by region.

4. The built vernacular heritage is an integral part of the cultural landscape, and this relationship must be taken into consideration in the development of conservation approaches.

5. The vernacular embraces not only the physical form and fabric of buildings, structures and spaces, but the ways in which they are used and understood, and the traditions and intangible associations which attach to them.

The charter also outlines crucial "guidelines in practice" which advises on how best to meet the principles of conservation of vernacular architecture. The topical issue of the adaptation of vernacular buildings to meet contemporary needs is one of the seven guidelines. "The adaptation and reuse of vernacular structures should be carried out in a manner which will respect the integrity of the structure, its character and form while being compatible with acceptable standards of living.[...]". The guidelines also recognise the need for up-skilling and training within the building and conservation sector, and for improving public awareness of vernacular architecture.

House-types in County Kildare

Thomas James Rawson described the typical farmyard complex in Kildare as follows: "the farm-houses in general consist of a long thatched building of one storey, containing a large kitchen and fire-place in the centre, and lodging rooms at either end; the front door looks to the barns and stables at the right, behind is the haggard, and on the left side are placed the cow and bullock houses".[2]

There are examples of such houses and farm complexes surviving today in County Kildare, however, this is but one of a number of house types that are quite distinct. The first coordinated official census of Ireland took place in 1841 and provides an historical view of the prevailing house types in Kildare in the nineteenth century. The census categorised four rural house types as follows:

Class one: Gentleman's residence
Class two: Larger farmhouses
Class three: Smaller farmhouses
Class four: Houses built of clay or perishable materials having only one room and window. Cabins of the very poor.

Of these categories, each of the four classes are represented in the current revised survey. The 1841 census documents that 3,846 class two houses existed in Kildare. This figure had risen by 666 the year of the next census, 1861. Of class three (smaller farm houses – the bulk of the structures to survive today), there was a dramatic reduction in the numbers from 9,323 to 7,296, a total reduction of 2,027. The greatest reduction in building numbers was the class four type, which reduced from 5,036 in number to 1,857, within twenty years, amounting to a 63% reduction. The impact of the famine must account, in part, for this dramatic reduction, even though it did not devastate Kildare to the same degree as other parts of Ireland. What is obvious from the statistical information is that the Famine all but wiped out the most vulnerable and destitute. Such was the impact on the population that it continued to decline until the establishment of the Free State. "The population of Leinster continued to fall until after the 1926 census… Leinster suffered less than most of the rest of the country. But, as a result, the amount of domestic building in the forty years after 1850 is comparatively small, so that we are largely spared a phase of development with which present taste is still out of sympathy."[3]

The rate of change shows clearly the rise in class two houses and the dramatic reduction in the levels of class four houses. This can be viewed as a general improvement of housing conditions during the second half of the nineteenth century, as well as a representation of the decline in numbers of the occupiers of the class four category house.

Fig. 2: A single-storey thatched farm house at Allenwood, Co. Kildare, which is nestled against the gentle slope of a field behind.

---

2. Rawson, Thomas James, *Statistical Survey of the County of Kildare, Dublin, 1807,* pp. 14-15.
3. Craig, Maurice, *The Personality of Leinster, Mercier Press, 1971.* p.61.

The following rather bleak description of the category four house-type, which was once a common sight in the raised bog areas of Kildare, illustrates, in great detail, the general form of the structure and how it was erected. It refers specifically to a description given to Reverend J. Hall, which he documents in *Tour Through Ireland*, providing a valuable indication of the domestic circumstances of the landless labourer class during the nineteenth century. It is this house category which saw such a dramatic reduction in the twenty years between the 1841 and 1861 census survey.

"I have a bog colony whose buildings are not of clay, but of turf, and very much varied; some attempt walls, with large blocks or squares of turf, which they commonly raise three or four feet; the common breadth of these tenements is about six feet, sometimes not above five; in these walls they place bog-sticks made fast at the angles with ropes of sedge; these timbers they cover with bog-sods, leaving a hole about the middle of the building for the smoke to escape; they use no thatch; they have no doors, nor door frames; the openings they secure with ill-jointed boards, which the families have had for perhaps half a century; they want no windows – when the bog-blocks or squares in the walls and on the roof dry, they have chinks and a free circulation of air through the whole building; they have neither pigs nor poultry, but their chief property is an ass, who in winter partakes of the advantage of their fireside, and the shelter of their cabin in common with the family.

Some of these huts are a mere excavation of the dry bog, and some are formed by placing bog timbers against the high banks and covered with sods, this saying that six out of the number have not the luxury of thatch." [4]

A rare example of such a structure was photographed early in the twentieth century on the bog in County Kildare. The habitation does not have an A-frame roof structure, but a simply formed covering lined with heather, or some herbage that was immediately available. It is the humblest of structures, without any hint of self-conscious, self-improvement, design or permanence. It is a primitive, yet reasonably efficient and natural response to an immediate need, that of seasonal habitation. It was erected, most likely, during the turf-cutting campaigns.

The distressing living conditions of the poorest inhabitants of County Kildare are confirmed by Samuel Lewis' *Topographical Dictionary of Ireland*. This also provides an important insight into a house-type which has been erased from the landscape.

"The circumstance and appearance of those of the population located on the bogs, or their immediate vicinity, are very unfavourable. On each side of those parts of the canal that pass through the bog the land is let in small lots to turf-cutters, who take up their residence on the spot, however dreary and uncomfortable. Their first care is to excavate a site for a habitation on the driest bank that can be selected, which is sunk so deep that little more than the roof is visible; this is covered with scanty thatch, or, more frequently, with turf pared from the bog, laid with the herbage upwards, which so perfectly assimilates with the aspect of the surrounding scenery that the eye would pass over it unnoticed, were it not undeceived by the appearance of children and domestic animals sallying from a hole in one side, and by the occasional gush of smoke from the numerous chinks in the roof." [5]

There were, of course, more permanent structures for the poor, which were slightly better than the earlier sod-built houses. The single-roomed cabin (see Fig. 3), which is nestled into the side of a hill, is a good example. This is a stone-built structure with a small chimney on the hill side. It appears to be direct-entry, and is lit internally by two small window openings. What is equally interesting is the outbuilding attached to the end of the house. It forms a temporary post and wattle byre and has a crude sod roof with tree branches fixed to its slopes forming stays which prevent what appears to be a herbage covering from falling away.

Ó Danachair says of such buildings: "Such a house, given a modest degree of prosperity for the occupants, could be neat and comfortable, while poverty and neglect could make it ill-kept and miserable". [6]

4. Hall, Rev. J, *Tour Through Ireland*, London 1813, Vol.1, p. 57.
5. Lewis, Samuel, *Topographical Dictionary of Ireland*, 1837, ii, p. 84.
6. JCKAS, 1966/67, p.235

Today, there are five main types of thatched houses surviving in County Kildare. The first of these is the thatched mansion, generally stone built, rising to two storeys in height and of quite early origin. The next category is the gentleman farmers' house, which is generally single-storey, semi-formal in design, with windows of Georgian proportions. The third type identified is the single-storey farm house with attendant farm buildings. Many are arranged to form a forecourt enclosed from the road by a simple boundary wall, while others form groups of buildings arranged in a more random configuration. The fourth type is the cottage within a site of limited scale (possibly former cotters houses), to which accretions have not generally been added. The final type is the crossroads-sited house which generally served a public function, such as the local forge, local shop, post office and public house. What survives today, though now quite limited in number when compared with 1987, is broadly representative of the thatched house-types found historically in Kildare. The notable exception is the impermanent hut or cabin, part covered excavation, part turf sod-walled structure, of which type no traces remain.

Type One: The Thatched Mansion

There are two surviving thatched mansions in County Kildare, a reduction of one from the three identified in the Higginbotham Survey of 1987. A thatched mansion is essentially a large two-storey thatched house, generally four bays or more across. It is widely understood that the thatched mansion developed from the seventeenth century. Caoibhín Ó Danachair points out that "another Irish building tradition possibly of medieval origin, which expressed itself in the 'thatched mansion', [was] the large two-storied thatched house which was common as the dwelling of prosperous farmers and lesser gentry in the 17th and 18th centuries, and which seems, in many cases to have been replaced by our typical Georgian mansion under the influence of the fashion of the later 18th century."[7]

The rareness of this typology adds to their significance. Ó Danachair has documented in detail the development of one particular thatched mansion in Kildare, Greatrath (see Fig. 4). In a discussion with the owner, Mr. Edmund Cleary, whose ancestors were in occupation of Greatrath since 1717, the development and changes to the structure were understood within the context of his ancestors' history. Such documentation, now nearly 50 years old, is an invaluable oral record of the history of one house.

According to Ó Danachair, each storey was "simply divided by a partition. Access to the upper storey was provided by a movable ladder through a trap door in the floor. The two upper rooms were bedrooms each of them had a fireplace in the gable wall. Each of the two ground floor rooms also had its fireplace: on the left of the door was the kitchen with its real open hearth and built-in oven, and on the right the other room, now used for general purposes, part store, part sitting room, part extra

Fig. 3: Image of cotter's house in County Kildare, courtesy of Department of Irish Folklore. (UCD. A015.09.00017)]

---

7. JCKAS, 1966/67, pp.243.

sleeping accommodation."[8] The use of bread ovens as documented in the foregoing passage has its origins in 17th century.[9] The bread oven, which had been blocked-up in the past, was uncovered in recent upgrading works to Greatrath. The oven survives and has proved a convenient conduit for plumbing provisions. A permanent stairs (with a gentle slope) was introduced, c.1770, against the internal partition wall in the middle of the house. This was in turn enclosed from the kitchen by a second partition, and this, with new windows, gave the house its present main internal form. The roof structure was replaced, c.1900, which resulted in the lowering of the wall at eaves level. It was intended at this time to cover the new roof with slate. Fortunately it was decided to re-thatch instead.

Fig. 5: The second thatched mansion in Greatrath, Co. Kildare

Fig. 4: Greatrath, Co. Kildare, an exceptionally fine example of the thatched mansion in the county.

Two thatched mansions are located within the townland of Greatrath, which is significant in light of the distribution of thatched houses within the county. It suggests a certain wealth associated with the townland and also on the part of the farmers who occupied both structures from the seventeenth century on-wards. A third thatched mansion identified by Higginbotham, in the townland of Boley Great, was demolished in 1992.

Type Two: The Gentleman's Farmhouse

This is also a rare typology within the county. It refers to single-storey thatched houses set apart from the vernacular by the gentlemanly pretensions of Georgian proportioned windows, fine volumetric qualities and architectural detailing internally. In each case, the house is accompanied by good sized ranges of stone outbuildings, and is set within fine grounds. The general form and architectural detailing suggests a date of c.1800 onwards. One such gentleman's farmhouse is The Hermitage, (Fig. 7) located within the townland of Boley Great, where the fine thatched mansion was demolished in 1992. Such fine structures located within the same townland further suggests the prosperity historically associated with the area. This includes Farrington's Stud (inventory no. 29) located near Jiggenstown in Naas.

Type Three: The Elongated House

This typology is perhaps the most plentiful in the county. In each case, the house is single-storey and ranges in size from three bays to seven bays in length. These are relatively large houses, which retain the one room deep plan common to all vernacular thatched buildings in the county. Each, to a greater or lesser

8. JCKAS, 1966/67, pp.243.
9. Sleeman, Mary, *Thatched Houses of County Cork*, Cork County Council, 2004, p. 16.

extent, represents a series of accretions and additions which have been added over time to accommodate the growing families and fortunes of its inhabitants. In most cases, extensions are easily identified by smaller chimneystacks to one or either end of the house, in addition to the large stout hearth chimneystack which formed the principal dividing wall before later additions. Irregular bonding of the extension (generally a one bay addition to one or both ends) to the original house is evident in many cases, which helps to indicate the evolution of the house. Another indicator is irregular fenestration, the smaller windows generally belonging to the earlier parts of the house. Kinks evident on the ridge and eaves should also help distinguish accretions. The setting and context of such houses is characterised by the placement of outbuildings perpendicular to the dwelling house, flanking it to either side, thus forming a forecourt, which is enclosed from the road by a low boundary wall. Less symmetrical and random placement of outbuildings has also been noted.

Fig. 6: (Top) The Hermitage, in the townland of Boley Great, Co. Kildare, appears to have been built between 1750-1800.
Fig. 7: (Above) Located at Thomastown Crossroads. Note the irregular placement of the windows, and the smaller chimneystack over the gable.

Fig. 8: (Left) This is the home of the thatcher Jack Donohue in Robertstown, which is attached to a building, possibly a local school at one point. This cottage, which retains much of its original character faces onto the canal towpath.

Fig. 9: (Below) McLoughlin's shop, at the end of a thatched house at Mountrice Crossroads, shares the junction with a wall mounted post box and Marian shrine.

Type Four: The Cottage on a Small Holding

This house type is quite rare and most houses originally of this type have been altered and extended over time. (Fig. 8) In each case, the cottage forms a three-bay single-storey house with a centrally placed door opening, and a simple two-roomed internal layout divided by the chimneybreast and jamb wall of the lobby entry. Extensions are generally located to the rear. Historically, these houses tend not to have outbuildings.

Type Five: Crossroads-sited Houses

There are a number of crossroads-sited houses that serve public functions. These may include the local forge, the local shop or public house. Each of these survives today in County Kildare. The importance of crossroads within the social infrastructure of rural communities is evident by the development of buildings of public use within close proximity. Crossroads are generally named – for instance Thomastown Crossroads, where a wall-mounted post box is inserted in the gate pier of a thatched house in private use – which signifies their importance within

the social dynamic of country life (see page 4). Other examples include the tin-roofed public house at Ballagh Crossroads, McLoughlin's shop at Mountrice Crossroads (Fig. 9), where a wall-mounted post box and Grotto dedicated to the Virgin Mary attribute importance to the junction. Close-by, at another junction, there is a forge, though it is no longer operational.

Type Six: New or Rebuilt Houses using Thatch

A number of new structures which interpret the vernacular style complete with thatched roofs, have been built in recent years in Kildare. There are some instances where a thatched house has been dramatically enlarged, such as that located at Painestown Crossroads, represented in Figs. 10/11. Originally a three-bay house with a single-storey addition to one side, this house, formerly known as O'Neill's shop, was prolonged by a single-storey single-bay addition linked to a dormer two-storey block breaking forward from the building line and set perpendicular to the original. Two thatched houses have been rebuilt using thatch.

The use of thatch in modern construction is to be welcomed for a number of reasons. First, it keeps the tradition alive, and where a growing demand exists, there will be thatchers with necessary skills. Secondly, the use of thatch in standard modern construction as a viable alternative to the prevailing roof covering should help to alter the perception of it as something antiquated. It should also promote the demand for thatching materials, a situation which requires much improvement.

Fig. 10: The house was dramatically enlarged when compared with the original.

Fig. 11: Formerly O'Neill's shop, located close to Painestown Crossroads, in its original form comprising a three bays single-storey house with a slate roofed single-bay addition.

Fig. 12: The hipped side elevation of a thatched house in Thomastown has a slight bow resulting in an arc at the eaves.

the pitch of the roof, leveling off just beneath the collar beams. The introduction of ceilings to interiors must have impacted on the thatching methodologies, which historically required some-one both inside and outside to receive the hemp rope used in local thatching. Today, of course, the rope is tied from without. Where original, each truss and collar beam is composed of roughly hewn (rather than sawn) timber from the boughs of trees which were normally locally or regionally sourced. However, according to one thatcher in County Kildare, the majority of roof structures are twentieth century replacements, and originals survive only rarely. In the preparation of this sur-vey there was limited access to roof structures. Where access was permitted, there was limited space in which to assess the form and type of the roof structure.

Examples of Roof Structures Surveyed

Fortunately it was possible to view the roof structure of four contrasting houses, one located by the Barrow Branch of the

The prevailing historic roof type of the thatched houses in County Kildare is the single-span, hipped roof, which is normal-ly pitched at a 40°-45° angle. The roof generally comprises quite a simple structure of A-framed principal rafter trusses with collar beams, set at regular intervals standing just beneath the top of the wall. This contrasts with more formal architecture where timber wall plates are generally employed to support the roof structure. This survey has identified at least one example where the roof truss has settled outside of the wall itself, an irregularity which adds to the interest of such a building.

There are also examples of gabled and half-gabled (or hipped-gabled) roof structures, found historically around the Kilcullen area. These are, however, the exception rather than the rule.

Historically, most thatch roof structures were exposed internal-ly. However, by the 1940s, most had been concealed behind timber-framed tongued and grooved ceilings, which followed

Fig. 13: The rough hewn A-framed timber roof structure of example one.

Grand Canal, another forming a modest three-bay cottage near Nurney, a now derelict farm house with a byre attached to one end, and an intact farm house where the byre forms an obvious extension to the original house. In both latter cases the roof structure remains exposed.

Example One:
This roof structure belongs to a rather handsome thatched house, ennobled by formally proportioned windows and a segmental-arched doorcase on the facade. The proximity of this house to the canal tow path would suggest that it was constructed after the opening of the canal and so may well date to the beginning of the nineteenth century. The roof space is accessible from the gabled side elevation where a replacement timber ladder rises to meet at attic opening. It is believed by the current owners that the attic space was historically used to accommodate farm hands. The roof structure forms the standard A-frame of principal rafter trusses, composed of roughly hewn timber, and strengthened by half round collar beams. One collar beam has scarring to suggest laths were once attached, which may have been reused from elsewhere, or may indeed have been used to partition the roof space. There is no underlying basal layer of

Fig. 15: The byre extension of this clay walled house has a sawn timber roof structure with the thatch placed directly onto purlins, to which it is attached with hemp rope.

scraw, and the thrust thatching technique appears to have been applied (note the jabs of knotted straw sticking out from the thatch).

Example Two:
This roof structure belongs to a modest three-bay two-roomed house, which was given a ceiling during the 1960s when the present owner acquired the property. The ceiling rises with the pitch of the roof before leveling off. The A-frame roof structure is composed of tree branches, the heavier forming the rafter trusses. The irregularity of the members indicates that the roofer was skilled in the use of local materials and could accommodate the imperfections of the raw material without compromising on the strength of the roof. Within the roof space, it was also possible to examine the chimneystack. The visible side of the chimneystack suggests it is a simple log timber framed flue shaft, lined with clay strengthened by wattle.

Example Three:
The V-shaped exposed truss-roof structure of this house, covers a byre which is located at one end of the now derelict house. The byre in this instance is a single-celled extension to one end

Fig. 14: Note the rope used to tie the thatch to the planked purlins. Note also the absence of a scraw.

of the house, leaving intact the original hip-roof of the house. The rear wall and side wall are composed of clay, while the front elevation wall appears to be formed of mass concrete. The trusses are composed of sawn timber and employ the use at least seven rows of purlins on each of the three sides. The purlins are more roughly formed than the trusses, to which they are attached on the outside. This is not a typical historical feature suggesting early twentieth century origins. The trusses of each A-frame rise directly from the clay walls just beneath the top which is flaunched with a rounded finish. The trusses rise to meet a sawn ridge board and are coupled at the hip ends for strength, and to form the rounded profile we associate with thatched roofs. There is no scraw of sod or any bedding material. The thatch is fixed to the roof structure by means of rope and scollops.

Example Four:
This roof structure is similar to the preceding roof structure in that it forms an extension to the main house. The original hip end survives, and can seen within the byre, where the roof struc-

Fig. 16: The roof of this structure of this byre extension incorporates the original hip-roof. Note the A-frame structure formed of roughly sawn timber, collar beams and purlins. Again there is no scraw and the thatched is bound to the roof by rope.

ture is entirely exposed. The A-frame roof structure is formed of sawn lengths of tree branch, the rough barked edges of which are evident on the purlins outside the A-frame. Again, there is no scraw and the thatch has been fixed to the purlins by means of rope and scollops. The rope may be an example of the hemp rope that was often used, though a bituminous coating, which the hemp rope was historically dipped in, was not noted.

Thatch Roof Covering
The local variations of thatching techniques and subtle signature features of local thatchers may, at first glance, go unnoticed. Idiosyncrasies in the thatching processes exist, which are often favoured by both thatcher and home-owner alike. Such differences were frequently known only locally. These locally emphasised processes were a legacy handed down orally by a master thatcher to his apprentice, often from father to son. Further uniqueness can be attributed to those households who thatched their own houses, though this no longer takes place in County Kildare. The range of thatching techniques employed in the county today may not reflect the historical variations that existed in preceding centuries. This is due to several factors. The limited number of surviving thatched structures naturally lessens the variations inherent within a large number of structures. The small number of thatchers in operation in the county has given way to greater homogeneity in techniques. In many cases, a thatcher may need to work within a number of counties to have a steady stream of work. The approach to each job may be one of expediency and efficiency, resulting in the loss of local variations. Therefore, we have moved from a local traditional emphasis to a regional one, which may, in time, become a provincial emphasis. The much diminished choice of thatching materials also limits the way in which the thatcher responds to a roof. Where once straw made from oats, wheat, rye, barley and bent was used, now only oaten straw is used. The historically unprecedented use of water reed for thatching in County Kildare is creeping in, albeit only in rare examples.

The most reliable source of information on the thatching techniques of County Kildare was compiled by the Irish Folklore Commission under the direction of Caoimhín Ó Danachair.[10] Ó Danachair coordinated the systematic gathering of information on many aspects of Irish rural life and folklore from the 1940s. This study is concerned with roofing and building materials. The information was gathered by sending questionnaires to individuals within each county. Responses tended to range from detailed analysis to simple yes/no answers. This information helps to build up an important historically accurate picture of thatching techniques from various points within the county before the advent of heavily mechanised harvesting and the use of chemical fertilizers, both of which have had a dramatic impact on thatching.

The questionnaire on roofing looked at a number of important factors, many of which help to define the regional varieties of thatching and roofing techniques within each county. The first question related to the form of the roof: whether it was hipped or gabled. The second question asked if a scraw existed under the thatch. The third question referred to the nature of the thatching material. The fourth question concerned the lifespan of a full rethatching. The fifth question asked whether the thatching was done by a professional thatcher or some other. The final question allowed for short descriptions of thatching techniques, some of which were more informative than others.

The following are verbatim accounts of the thatching techniques archived by the Irish Folklore Commission:

"• Remove fatigued outer layers until a substrate of 'fairly dry straw' is found.
• A handful of straw has some of itself twisted round the top. That is thrust in close to another by making a hole with a thatching stick. When all is finished scollaps [sic] of sally hazel, snow-drop woods are put on over the thatch.
• Straw is arranged on the ground by a handler into bundles 'the width of a ladder' and are given to the thatcher who places two at at time starting at the eaves and working upwards. Each bundle is doused with water and treated with a rake.
• Hazel scallops [sic] are used to fix the thatch to the substrate material.
• In addition stitches it with twine. (There used to be special thatching twine as thick as a pencil which had been steeped in a bituminous solution. This is no longer available and synthetic bailing twine is the working substitute).
• Bobbins of straw are worked along the ridge to achieve a finished appearance and prevents ingress.
• Some kind of plant is full grown on some houses to prevent the house from going on fire. I saw this in County Limerick too.
• Spraying thatch with bluestone gives a lovely colour and preserves thats and kills ...seeds and kills insects and keeps away birds."[11]
"• Thatching a house already thatched you use a thatching fork like a two grained fork but smaller.
• Use straw as long as possible in strokes [sic] and they put the fork in the middle of the straw and put it into the old thatch.
• They put one end under the straw and leave the other end hang down. They always start at the bottom.
• Scollops are made from 'sally' sticks and both ends of them are pointed and secured.
• 'Scollops' are only put at the top of the roof.
• After thatching water is splashed on it to tighten the straw and then it is raked down evenly with a thatching rake.
• Bluestone [copper sulphate] dissolved in water is applied after this with sprayer.
• When all this is finished the thatcher cuts the eaves, to make them even, with a sheers and they leave them about a foot long."[12]
"• When the dwelling house is not ceiled inside the thatch has to be stitched. The thatcher uses a needle a foot long thread-

10. The School of Irish, Celtic Studies, Irish Folklore and Linguistics at UDC kindly provided access to the extensive records compiled by Ó Danachair, which informs much of this section.
11. IFC questionnaire completed by Seán ó Clúnain, O.S.Allenwood NS Robertstown, Naas.
12. IFC questionnaire competed by Pádraig Ua h-Arachtáin (Patrick Harrington)Roberstown.

ed with binder twine, when he puts on the bundle of straw he fastens it with a loop of binder twine, a man inside draws the needle in and catches the loop round a rafter and passes the needle out again to the thatcher on the roof.

- When the house is ceiled one foot long hazel twigs pointed at both ends called scallops are fastened round the bundles of straw to fasten them into the roof. The bundle of straw is driven in by a tool like a large awl.
- When a new roof of thatch has to be put on for the first time a thick rope called a collaic is drawn tightly along the top of the house to which the bundles of straw are fastened when the thatcher begins to cover the roof.
- The dressing of straw roofs with bluestone makes the thatch last 4 or 5 years longer."[13]

Observations on the thatching techniques and the questionnaires issued by Ó Danachair were usually prepared by the local head master, school teacher, or parish priest, who relayed and often dictated information from local thatchers and home owners at first hand. The following are two differing variations in the thatching tradition recorded in County Kildare.

"There are two methods in use in these districts [Athy]. One method is a handful of straw is taken and a sort of knot is formed on the straw at one end and this is trust [sic] in with an implement which the thatcher calls a (truster) [sic] a short iron spike with a short wooden handle. Scallops (hazel sticks) are used only at the top of the roof. There are three rows of hazel sticks or scallops placed on each side of the top of the roof. The handful of straw which the thatcher trusts in is called a (fangle) of straw. The second method is each handful of straw is laid on in rows about a yard wide and confined to the roof with scallops. The thatcher that uses the former method is considered the best thatcher."

Always before the house is thatched a considerable portion of the thatch or straw is removed from the roof. If the old thatch is very much damaged, the new layer of straw or thatch has to be sown on with a large needle and "thatching cord". The thatcher remains on the outside of the roof and a helper puts the needle through inside and then pushes the needle out to the thatcher again and continues this until the whole roof is covered.[14]

The Use of Scraw

The use of scraw has been identified as an important part of the thatching tradition in Ireland. The scraw was generally formed of a herbage such as sods of grass or heather, which acts as an underlay spread over all the roof structure. The thatched layers were built up on the scraw and anchored to it using scollops.

This survey has not identified any scraw basal layers to roof structures that have been inspected. It would appear that the use of scraw in traditional thatching had all but died out by the time of the Irish Folklore Commission questionnaires were carried out. One person questioned replied that "there was up some [scraw] 50 or 60 years ago. Since then this practice has been discontinued and has been superseded by using this thatching needle and cord." Another respondent maintained that, "Nowadays, when no scraws are used the thatch is sewn onto the timber wood of the roof – the thatcher being on the roof while his assistant is engaged inside to take charge of the stitching cord, which he puts round the longitudinal lathing."[15]

The reason scraw is no longer used in County Kildare is not understood. It was most likely discontinued when the majority of roof structures were replaced during the first decade of the twentieth century.

13. IFC questionnaire completed by Mrs. Helen Mitchell, Kilkcaskin, Carbury, Co. Kildare.
14. IFC questionnaire completed by Sara Rowan (N.T.), Kilberry NS, Athy, Co. Kildare.
15. IFC questionnaire completed by Mrs. Michael Flaherty/Mr. Michael Hynes (Stonemason), Castledermot, (71 yrs) who furnished this information.

The Eaves

The eaves are generally angled at 45° with a 300 mm-500 mm overhang, which terminates with a drip course formed by lowering the outermost layer of thatch. The eaves are a crucial detail of the roof structure, designed to throw rainwater off the roof away from the wall surface, thus keeping it dry. If the eaves are not deep enough and conversely too heavy, they will be at risk of decay. Failing eaves will sag with the weight of rain, and begin to decay according to Jack Donohue, a well known local thatcher. Once the eaves begin to decay, houses constructed with clay walls are at imminent risk.

The Ridge

The ridge of a thatched roof is generally where subtle design flourishes exist. It must be stressed, however, that the Irish thatching tradition is not very decorative. Prominent features such as the twisted or roped ridge with bobbins (raised knots) and rows of scollops appear decorative, but the design, while aesthetically pleasing, is crucial to maintaining a watertight ridge. Chimneystacks normally rise from the ridge forming plain stout rendered shafts with cement flaunching surrounding the base where it meets the thatch roof.

Fig. 17: (Above): The sloping eaves of a thatched roof.

Fig. 18: The twisted or plaited finish to the ridge of a house in Kildare. Note the bobbin to the end and the rows of scolloping.

TIN ROOF STRUCTURES

The use of metal as a roof covering actually began during the second half of the nineteenth century. Corrugated iron was developed in Britain in 1829, when it was realised that iron rolled into a series of regular corrugations was stronger, weight for weight, than flat iron sheets. This offered considerable savings in the quantity of metal required, and in the covering of roofs. The catalyst for the use of corrugated metal sheeting as a cladding material to steel or timber framed structures was the need for accommodation constructed in an expedient manner. This is nowhere more obvious than in Australia and New Zealand, where a rush of immigrants from Europe required shelter. In Ireland, foundries such as Kennan's of Fishamble Street had designed sanitoria and timber-framed corrugated metal-faced housing for export and for domestic use. Corrugated metal exists in a number of quite important buildings throughout Ireland. When it became a viable option for home owners in Ireland has not been discovered by this writer.

Galvanized corrugated iron was also developed by the middle of the nineteenth century and rapidly became the most widely used roofing material. Its advantages are that it is easily and swiftly applied (even by unskilled labour). It is light, compact, inexpensive, fireproof and immune from insect attack. Its use was encouraged when enough iron to cover the roof of a cottage could be transported easily when flat packed, making a load that was light enough to be dragged over poor roads to almost any building site.

The terms "corrugated iron" and "galvanized iron" became misnomers after about 1915 when steel began to replace iron in the manufacturing process. The change went unnoticed by the general public, which continued to refer to "corrugated iron" and "galvanized iron". The use of the word tin is no less accurate, but has found its way into the parlance of vernacular architecture.

Fig. 19: This tin-roofed structure in Kildoon was put over the existing thatched roof since 1988.

The use of tin roofing material on domestic vernacular buildings, superseding the use of thatch, was an economic and practical choice. The reasons for its introduction are obvious. Galvanized metal roofing requires far less maintenance and cyclical renewal (8-10 years for a well thatched roof) is not a burden. The initial outlay of erecting a light timber roof structure over the existing thatch roof, to carry the tin covering, was widely recognized as an economically logical decision.

This survey has identified 58 tin-roofed houses in County Kildare, a figure broadly equal to the number of extant thatched buildings. The large number of tin-roofed houses add significantly to the heritage of thatched properties in the county, notwithstanding the reality that what survives today is but a glimpse of what was once a regular sight within the rural landscape. The importance of tin-roof structures (most likely all formerly thatched) cannot be over-estimated.

In most cases, the tin covering has been applied to an outer timber-frame, which has been built over the existing thatched roof structure. While examination of tin roofed structures was outside the remit of this study, some of the thatched houses included in the Higginbotham survey have since been covered by tin and it was possible to get information from owners. The general practice of erecting a tin-covered roof structure over an existing thatched roof structure formed, in effect, a double roof. The underlying thatched roof structures of most of these houses are amongst the oldest surviving examples of thatch material in the county. In each case, the thatch material has not been renewed since the erection of the tin roof structure. In some cases this thatch may be over 50 years old, forming important material evidence of the thatching techniques and materials no longer available or practiced.

Corrugated steel is also becoming an increasingly important material which contributes to the broad range of structures and building technologies recognised as part of the architectural heritage of the country. As such, the maintenance and survival of tin roofs should be encouraged.

Fig. 20: The tin has been removed from the roof of Silliot Lodge (demolished in 1987), which was located on the road from Kildare to Kildangan. The simple A-frame roof structure was placed over the existing thatched roof. In many cases the chimneystacks have to be built up to take the additional ridge height. (image courtesy of Irish Folklore Department, UCD, A024.09.00049)

The two prevailing historical construction methods identified in County Kildare are broadly in line with other counties where the availability of stone is rare, traditionally making it a very expensive building material. By contrast, clay was extremely cheap and readily available.

Building Characteristics of Clay-built Houses

The following are the principal characteristics which aid the identification of a clay-walled house. These are by no means definitive but prove helpful on site. Asking the owners if they are aware of the construction of the house is also important for clarification. The characteristics are:

- Lime rendered clay walls built on basal layer of stone.
- Lime rendered clay walls built directly on ground.
- Battered or irregular corners.
- Engaged buttressing, all occurring with clay-built houses.

The following is a description of the process by which clay walled houses are constructed and the geographical distribution of them in Ireland.

"...Tempered clay was also an excellent walling material provided that the clay was properly prepared and applied. A basal layer of stones underneath the clay was desirable as a foundation for the building, and for protecting the base of the clay walls from dampness. It was also necessary for the outer surface of the clay walls to be suitably rendered to protect them from the weather. A generous overhang to the thatched eaves, to prevent water from the roof dripping onto the walls underneath, was also a necessity. Clay houses are found mainly in the drier east and southeast of Ireland. The vast majority of clay buildings are one-storey in height, though two-storey, or multi-storey buildings of clay, or partly constructed of clay, are also found. The walls can be up to a metre thick, and in the south and east of Ireland they were normally constructed to wall-head height on which a hipped roof with four sloping sides was placed." [16]

Clay-wall constructed houses are praised for their thermal properties. They are warm in winter and cool in summer. Many owners preferred the internal atmospheric conditions of the clay-walled house rather than the late twentieth century extensions, which were criticized for being too hot in summer and too cold in winter!

Fig. 21: This clay-walled side elevation has been incorporated within a byre extension. The base of the wall has been built up with a protective layer of rubble stones to prevent damage to the clay wall from animals. The stone facing has partly fallen away taking with it the lime render coating, exposing the clay of the wall.(Site no. 16)

Though when properly constructed clay houses are every bit as permanent as stone-built houses, there are exceptionally vulnerable, if a property is not properly maintained. Clay walls, like

---

16. Lysaght, Patrick, *Vernacular Rural Dwellings in Ireland*, Dept of Irish Folklore, UCD, p.15.

every other type of construction, require water-tight conditions to function properly. This is why an outer coating of render is applied, and also why the eaves are so deep, throwing water off away from the walls. When thatch fatigues or is not replaced the threat of decay sets in. Once water ingress becomes constant, the clay-walled house will virtually disintegrate in a short period of time.

Building Characteristics of Stone-Built Houses

The construction of the stone-built house required more precision which is reflected in the more regularised angles and wall surface. Rendering, particularly with thick layers of modern cement render, makes it virtually impossible to detect the stone construction underneath. Like clay-walled houses, the stone used generally comes from a local source. However the lack of availability of stone and the time and skill required to construct such a house would have made it very expensive, when compared with clay-walled construction. The geographical distribution of surviving stone-built thatched houses in Kildare appears to be rather random, as they are not located near any notable sources of stone. The use of stone does not always suggest high profile buildings as it is used for both thatched mansions and modest cottages. Stone is also used in conjunction with clay, and such houses are described as part-clay constructed. A number of these buildings also survive.

The survival rate of stone-built houses compared with clay-constructed houses is striking. It is not clear if the substantial loss of clay-walled houses is exclusively a result of the rapid deterioration process in neglected properties, or if the typology was less regarded than stone-built houses.

The characteristics of stone built houses are: rendered rubble-stone construction; regular squared elevations; the absence of a batter.

Fig. 22: (Above) This clay walled house in Turnakill, is now a ruin and will be, in a short space of time, virtually untraceable. Note the country style dresser which still stands inside though the thatched roof and clay walls around it have disintegrated.

Fig. 23: (Right) The coursed rubblestone of this house in Walterstown relies on regular angles and plumb lines for the stability of the construction. Only traces of the lime render coating of this house remain. Note also the stone sills, which are roughly hewn, and scarcely have enough of a projection to throw water off. It is therefore no surprise to find that most of the sills recorded are remade in cast cement.

The interiors of the thatched houses in County Kildare are characterised by two main types, the direct-entry house and the lobby entry house. The direct-entry house is obvious from the exterior when the main hearth chimneystack and main entrance are at opposite ends of the kitchen. By contrast the lobby entry is generally aligned, or placed just to the side of the main hearth chimneystack. Floor plans in almost all cases are one-room deep, with the basic plan comprising of an open-hearth kitchen, the hearth chimneybreast separating the second room which is accessed through an opening to one side of the jamb wall. Each is lit by one window, and in many cases there is a second door providing rear access from the kitchen. From this basic template various permutations arise, generally in the form of one or two rooms located at either or both ends of the house separated by the original external wall, or simple timber framed partitions. Some accretions are added to form L-plans, but these tend to be much later additions, perhaps c. 1900.

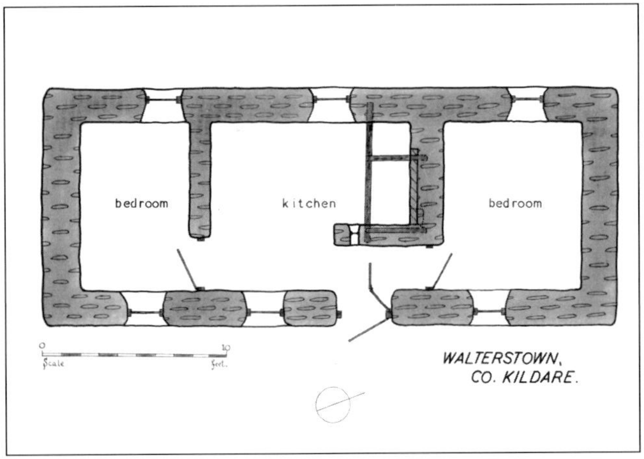

The hearth chimneybreast is essentially a transverse load-bearing wall which supports the roof structure internally.

The hearth is one of the main principal structural and formal elements within the thatched house. It is both the social and domestic centre of the house, where stories are shared, food is cooked, and the inhabitants are warmed. The hearth wall traverses the house and generally runs to approximately a metre in depth.

The hearth canopy oversails the open fire and forms a large chamber through which smoke is funnelled out of the house. Most of the canopies viewed in this survey were vertical, not sloped as is the case with the example in Fig. 25. The canopy is usually a clay wattle structure supported by a timber beam, one end of which is embedded in the rear wall of the house, while the other end is embedded in the jamb wall which forms the partition for the lobby.

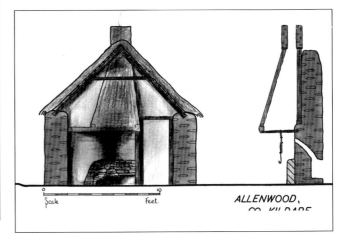

Fig. 24: A typical floor plan of a three-bay lobby entry house with a central kitchen defined by the hearth. A bedroom is located at either end. Note the double hinged door which folds back to allow unobstructed access to the bedroom on the right. (Image courtesy of the Irish Folkore Department, UCD A015.09.00868)

Fig. 25: This diagram represents two sections of a house in Allenwood Co. Kildare, one of the houses showing the elevation of the hearth, and the other a section through the hearth. (Image courtesy of the Irish Folkore Department, UCD A021.09.00023)

Fig. 26: An internal partition wall, in this case, not a hearth wall, but nonetheless illustrating the incorporation of the A-frame of the roof structure in the wall.

Fig. 27 A traditional hearth with a nineteenth century range built into the open hearth and incorporating a wrought-iron crane.

The hearth wall rises to include one of the principal rafter trusses of the A-frame roof structure. This forms a reinforcing frame for the wall, which is also intended as a secondary support for the roof structure. (see Fig. 26). The chimney flue forms a timber framed structure, which is lined with wattle that is then given a coating of render. The timber-constructed canopy and flue is a vernacular tradition practiced for generations. It has been suggested that because of the size of the flue void, and the circulation of cool air within the flue, the temperature reduces inside quite dramatically, reducing the risk of fire. Hearth walls are sometimes twinned by a secondary fireplace on the opposing wall to heat the bedroom. In many cases, this simply forms an angled tunnel through the clay wall until the main hearth flue is reached.

Generally speaking, the hearths which have been inspected remain largely intact. Some, however, have been blocked up to form normal-sized openings to accommodate a range, or they have been blocked up altogether. Where they do survive many retain the wrought-iron crane and associated hardware. Generally, the hardware is not operational and has been retained for nostalgic and decorative reasons.

The lobby entry

The lobby entry is also a seminal feature of the vernacular tradition and many have been found to survive intact. The lobby is partitioned from the kitchen by the jamb wall of the hearth which is punctured by a spy window. The jamb wall prevents drafts blowing against the hearth which would cause smoke to enter the kitchen. The spy window allowed the inhabitant to see who was entering the house while at the same time providing much needed daylight to the hearth area, where much of the cooking took place.

The half-door

The necessity for keeping the front door open may well have led to the development of the half-door. It is generally a plank or tongued-and-grooved timber door leaf. Sometimes the main door is halved and in other cases a separate half-door leaf is hinged to the door jamb on the outside. This could remain closed while the full-length door stayed open. The full-length door leaf always opens inwards. The plan in Fig. 24 shows a door leaf which is double-hinged allowing for the door to fold back on itself, thus preventing the obstruction of the passage to the end room of the house behind the hearth chimney wall. None, however, were noted during this survey.

Many of the thatched houses surveyed were sited within small farmyards. Others, not in farm use, often have a single outbuilding, or a small range of sheds. Many of the farm buildings noted were composed of stone, while the farm house was composed of clay. This may seem strange, and could be explained by a number of factors. Vernacular houses in the county for the most part were composed of clay, which was preferred for its cheapness, availability, and thermal qualities. It is often observed that a farm house is secondary in scale and "quality" to the surrounding farm buildings. They were the infrastructure that sustained the economic stability of the family.

The perception today of the two prevailing building materials for vernacular structures, stone and clay, seem to favour stone, not so much for its durability, but for its status. This perception may not have existed during earlier centuries.

The arrangement of farm buildings can be both symmetrically and asymmetrically disposed, such as that represented in Fig. 29. The diagram shows an example of a farm plan, surveyed by the Irish Folklore Department, UCD, in 1935. Unlike the underlying principle and the desire for aesthetic effect which informed the symmetrical layout, this apparently haphazard plan is more an organic response to the reality of farming. The buildings are clustered so that a gate hung from the corner of one outbuilding closed against another, resulting in a flexible system of farm animal management. Note how buildings are huddled near the house, perhaps suggesting the limited holding of the farmer, but also suggesting a desire for convenience. It is also notable that the hen shed is closest to the house, the tending of which traditionally has been the female role. Together, the farm buildings exceed the dwelling house in scale, again suggesting the extent of the holding of livestock required to sustain a family in rural Ireland.

Fig. 28: A half-door which is separate from this handsome raised and fielded panel led timber front door which leads into a lobby entry house.

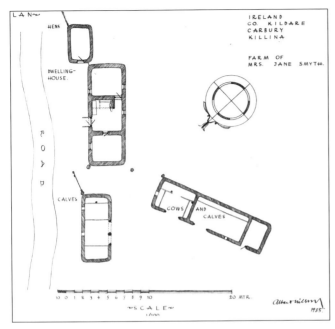

Fig. 29: Farmyard plan surveyed in 1935 in Carbury. (A030.09.00001)

The Perception of Thatched Houses Today

Today, the picturesque quality of thatch has appealing aesthetic value for the passer-by. In Kildare, thatched houses tend to be meticulously maintained and many owners take great pride in the appearance of their property and the contribution that thatched houses make to the heritage and tourism market of the county. As the number of thatched houses dwindles, their aesthetic and cultural value appears to be increasing.

The growing rarity and irreplaceable nature of vernacular architecture, like all aspects of heritage which is under threat, is being appreciated by more and more people. Thatched houses and farm buildings were a pragmatic response to local traditions, the surrounding environment, the availability of materials, prevailing weather conditions and economic factors. Aesthetics were not a primary consideration, yet the general response to them is one of aesthetic appreciation. The growth in recent decades of house building in the countryside which is distinctly suburban in character also amplifies the uniqueness of thatched houses. What were once unself-conscious dwellings along roadsides and down boreens, are now unique objects in the rural landscape to be admired and appreciated by all.

With the introduction of bungalow pattern books during the 1960s and '70s, thatched houses were all but abandoned. New "modern" bungalows were built to replace them, which were often constructed in front of the older house. The old thatched house was then converted to an outbuilding or allowed to disintegrate entirely. An attitude soon developed which viewed thatched houses as symbols of rural poverty and destitution. This now appears to be reversing. The 2005 Thatch Survey has identified four cases where thatched houses were chosen, all by young families, in which to live.

Fig. 30: The relationship between the dairy and the single-storey range of outbuildings proves important in the movement of animals into and out of the farm yard. The wrought-iron gate with characteristic arched brace bar and decorative c-scrolls are typical of these farm gates.

Collinstown

Detached five-bay single-storey lobby-entry thatched house, built c.1800, with a modern extension to the rear. Hipped oaten straw thatched roof having a twisted ridge with exposed scolloping to ridge and bobbins to either end; centrally placed rendered chimneystack with a terracotta pot. Pebble dash rendered clay walls with a smooth rendered plinth course of approximately 60cm in thickness. Square-headed window openings, uPVC windows, and concrete sills. Square-headed door opening set in a projecting windbreaker, with a uPVC door opening onto a concrete step. This well-maintained house is located on a prominent crossroads making it a well known feature of the landscape.

Drehid

Detached three-bay lobby-entry thatched house, built c.1800. Hipped oaten straw thatched roof having a twisted ridge with exposed scollops and decorative bobbins to either end. Centrally placed whitewashed rendered chimneystack. Whitewash over rough-cast render clay walls of approximately 60cm in thickness, and a smooth render plinth course to all elevations. Square-headed window openings, smooth render surrounds, rough stone sills, retaining some single-pane timber sash windows. Square-headed door opening set in a windbreaker; tongued-and-grooved timber door leaf. Probably one of the most intact thatched houses in the county, retaining a multitude of external features not usually found on a single structure. This house and its most attractive setting is a great example of the thatched vernacular tradition.

Moortown

Detached four-bay single-storey lobby-entry thatched house (formerly O'Neill's shop), built c.1850, much enlarged by a single-bay slated accretion to west and a single-bay two-storey thatched section to east, built c.2000 and a single-storey thatched return to rear. Pitched oaten straw thatched roof to the four-bay section, hipped to the two-storey section, both with twisted ridges and exposed scollops. Rendered chimneystack. Rough cast and pebble-dashed rendered walls. Square-headed window openings with concrete sills; one forming bracketed timber sill. Single pane timber sash windows to the original section with two-over-two timber sash windows to the new sections having horns. Square-headed door opening with tongued-and-grooved timber door and heritage style door furniture, opening onto concrete step.

Ballynagappagh

Detached five-bay single-storey direct-entry thatched house, built c.1800, with a windbreaker entrance porch and a lean-to return. Hipped oaten straw thatched roof with a twisted and scolloped ridge. Two rendered chimneystacks with clay pots. Natural slate to windbreaker. Rough cast rendered clay walls with a rendered plinth course. Single-pane timber sash windows. Flat-panelled timber shutters visible to interior. Modern timber panelled door. Tongued-and-grooved timber half-door to rear. Set perpendicular to the road with a large front site, and large farmyard to rear. Good example of the thatched house extended over time in a linear fashion to form a long house. This working farmhouse with its extensive farmyard retains all its external features and is of considerable aesthetic value.

Loughanure Commons

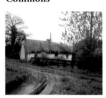

Detached three-bay single-storey lobby-entry thatched house, built c.1800. Oaten straw thatched roof, hipped to the west and gabled to the east. Twisted scolloped ridge. A central rendered chimneystack and a further stack rising from the east gable with a clay pot. Battered whitewashed rendered clay walls. Square-headed window openings with concrete sills and two-over-two timber sash windows. One window opening to the rear. Square-headed door opening with a tongued-and-grooved timber door. Located perpendicular to a narrow boreen. Appears intact with flat-panelled timber shutters and a flagstone floor.

Curryhills

Detached three-bay single-storey formerly thatched house, built c.1800. Front entrance porch added c.1950. Re-roofed c.1990. Pitched corrugated iron roof with a small rendered chimneystack and cast-iron rainwater goods. Rendered clay walls approximately 1m in thickness. Square-headed window openings with bipartite fixed pane timber windows. A six-pane timber casement window to the rear is recessed to the interior wall. Tongued-and-grooved timber door to the rear. This modest scale cottage has had its thatched roof replaced or covered over yet still retains some original windows. Now vacant, the house will soon fall into a ruinous state.

Curryhills	Allenwood	Allenwood North	Robertstown	Landestown	Millicent South

Curryhills

Original house demolished c.1995 and surrounding lands used for a housing development. Pastiche replacement thatched house built replacing original forming a detached five-bay single-storey thatched house built c.1995. Hipped oaten thatched roof, with conspicuously steep and angular pitch; rendered chimneystack. Painted cement rendered walls. Single-pane timber sash windows. Tongued-and-grooved timber half-door.

Allenwood

Detached five-bay single-storey lobby-entry thatched house, built c.1800, byre added to the east, c.1900, and a front entrance porch, c.1950. Windows enlarged, c.1980. Hipped oaten straw thatched roof with a twisted and scolloped ridge, bobbins to either end. Roof constructed of rough-sawn A-frame timbers with straw rope binding. Roughcast render over clay walls. Clay and rubblestone to east gable wall. Square-headed window openings with rendered reveals and timber casement windows to front c.1950; two-over-two timber sash windows to rear. Replacement timber panelled door and sidelights. Lobby entry with spy hole and an open hearth with iron hearth hardware. Tongued-and-grooved timber panelled ceiling. Concrete floors throughout. Set perpendicular to the road at a crossroads with a walled front site containing outbuildings.

Allenwood North

Detached six-bay single-storey thatched house, built c.1800. Hipped oaten thatched roof over a sawn timber roof structure with exposed scollops to the ridge and the eaves tied with straw. Whitewashed clay walls. Square-headed window openings with two-over-two timber sash windows and concrete sills. An earlier six-over-three timber sash window to the rear. Set parallel to the road at a lower level and obscured by growth.

Robertstown

Attached three-bay single-storey thatched house, built c.1800. Entrance porch added c.1950. Flat-roof extension to rear, built c.1980. Attached to a stone two-storey building along the Grand Canal. Pitched oaten straw thatch roof with twisted scolloped ridge. Concrete coping to gables. Central rendered chimneystack with clay pot. Painted rendered clay walls. Square-headed window openings with concrete sills and two-over-two timber sash windows with exposed sash boxes. Two-pane timber casement window to porch. Simple direct-entry floor plan comprising two rooms divided by large formerly open hearth chimneybreast. Doubled in size with extension to rear, built c. 1990. Paved front site. Located parallel to Grand Canal tow path.

Landestown

Detached four-bay single-storey thatched house, built c.1850, facing southwest with a flat-roofed projecting entrance porch and a two-bay tin-roofed section attached to the south. Single-storey extension to rear, c. 1940. Oaten straw thatched roof, hipped to the west and gabled to the east with a central brick chimneystack. Pebbledash render over rubble stone walls. Square-headed window openings with painted concrete sills and uPVC windows. Position of chimneystack in line with front door opening suggests this may have been a lobby entry floor plan. Simple floor plan with one room to either side of the hearth, prolonged to one side by an additional single-bay room.

Millicent South

Detached five-bay single-storey house, c.1800, with two bays to north, c.1850. Fell into dereliction, c.1990. Since rescued. Rebuilt section to west elevation. Oaten thatched roof and new roof structure re-covered in 2005. Square-headed window openings with concrete sills to west. Rescued from dereliction and currently being restored by owner, re-roofed in oaten straw thatch. Exposed rubble limestone walls, with traces of lime render surviving. Alterations to interior floor plan including rebuilding of structurally unsound chimneystack. Admirable project breathing new life into this property. New dormer two-storey extension to west side currently under construction.

Barretstown

The original house has been demolished and rebuilt, c.2004-2005, on a vastly larger scale. Oaten thatch roof with scolloped ridge. Rendered walls. Small square-headed window openings, with timber sash windows. Plank timber doors. Large site, with a multiple of outbuildings, all of which are modern.

Stickens

Detached four-bay single-storey house, built c.1800, with porch added c.1980, single-storey extension, added c.1990. Oaten thatch hipped-gabled roof with scollop ridge. Single rendered chimneystack. Pitched pan tiled roof to extension, intersecting rear span of thatched roof. Rendered rubblestone walls. Small square-headed window openings, enlarged c.1990, with timber casement windows. Lobby entry floor plan with single-bay room to either side of the hearth chimneybreast, prolonged by additional room to side of former kitchen. Hardwood timber door. Once facing onto the "old road", replaced c.1950, when the "new road" was laid and redirected away from the house.

Cloncumber

(Bally Tiegue Castle) Detached five-bay single-storey former lobby-entry thatched house, built c.1850, with a single-bay single-storey brick/stone return. Oaten straw thatched roof, gabled to east, hipped to west; twisted ridge and bobbin to ends; rendered chimneystack to centre and gable. A-frame roof structure of rough-sawn rafters and collars formed from natural tree sections, purlins fixed to the outer side. Rough-cast rendered clay and stone walls, c.67cm deep. Timber casement windows, c.1980. Doorcase comprising timber pilasters and console brackets with lintel architrave and elliptical overlight; flat-panelled timber door leaf. Opens onto a limestone step and a cobbled front area. Parallel to the road and the Grand Canal tow path, at a bend in the road.

Thomastown

Detached three-bay single-storey thatched house, built c.1750, facing northeast, with two-bay single-storey extension perpendicular to rear, c.1980. To the northwest is a further detached two-bay single-storey clay-walled former barn. Hipped oaten straw thatched roof with a central rendered chimneystack. Painted ruled-and-lined rendered battered clay walls. Square-headed window openings with hardwood casement windows. Square-headed central door opening with hardwood timber panelled door. Lobby entry house forming simple floor plan of a single-bay room either side of a massive formerly open-hearth chimneybreast. Small thatched outbuilding, quite ornamental in style, with an oaten thatched roof. Former barn to the northwest with a pitched corrugated iron roof.

Thomastown

Detached six-bay single-storey thatched house, built c.1800, facing east with a single-storey return to rear and lean-to outbuilding to west; north bay forms nineteenth century accretion. Oaten straw thatched roof, hipped to the south, gabled to the north. Roughcast rendered chimneystack to centre and to north gable. Corrugated-iron roof return. Roughcast render over rubble stone walls. Square-headed window openings with timber casement windows, c.1990. Timber sash window to rear. Modern hardwood timber panelled door. Gravelled front yard enclosed by white-washed rubblestone walls, with gate piers and wrought-iron gates to Morristown Road junction. Cast-iron V.R. wall-mounted post box.

Naas West

Detached four-bay single-storey thatch house, built c.1700, (formerly Farrington's Stud) with an Edwardian two-bay two-storey accretion to rear. Porch, c.1950. Oaten thatch roof with blind scollop ridge. Chimneystacks rebuilt c.1960. Ruled and lined rendered clay constructed walls. Rendered north and south gables. South-facing gable with projecting chimneybreast, with weather slate coping. One-over-one timber sash windows. Square-headed door opening, with flat panelled timber door leaf. Located on substantial site. Rubble limestone and brick outbuildings with loft having granite and limestone quoins; granite date plaque to one reads: 1890. Site enhanced by low slung outbuilding to northeast. Fine structure adding significantly to heritage of town and county.

Baltracey

Detached four-bay single-storey thatched house, built c.1850, with an attached single-bay lofted section built after1987; prolonged by tin-roof structure to enclose a front yard. Pitched oaten straw thatched roof with a twisted ridge with scollops. Replacement cement rendered chimneystack to centre and one to south gable. Pebble dash rendered walls, 60cm deep. Timber casement windows having simple wrought-iron bars set into the sills. Replacement tongued-and-grooved timber door beneath overlight with metal grille. Site enclosed by rubblestone walls terminated to the north by a high cement block wall. Stream with stone bridge to south.

Ummeras More

Detached four-bay single-storey thatched house, built c.1800. Well executed and integrated four-bay single-storey extension to rear, built c.1995. Hipped oaten straw thatched roof with a twisted ridge and hazel scollops to the ridge and eaves and bobbin to either end. Rendered chimneystack. Lime washed rough-cast render clay walls with a plinth course to the front elevation and two buttresses. Irregularly sized window openings with splayed reveals and timber casement windows and no sills. Door set in projecting windbreaker, with tongued-and-grooved door. Beautifully set in the landscape facing west parallel to the Grand Canal below the level of the Canal bank.

Quinsborough

Detached five-bay single-storey lobby-entry thatched house with windbreaker entrance return, c.1830. Attached outbuilding to west and a further range of outbuildings set perpendicular to the front. Gabled oaten straw roof with twisted and scolloped ridge. Two rendered chimneystacks with clay pots. Corrugated-iron roof to the return. Rough-cast render over rubble limestone walls. Two-over-two timber sash windows. Windbreaker incorporated under the deep eaves of the thatch roof covering; tongued-and-grooved timber door. Interior appears intact with flat-panelled timber shutters. Good rubble limestone outbuildings forming forecourt enclosed from road by a rendered wall, with wrought-iron gates. Fine house with a grandness setting it apart from the norm.

Mullaghroe Lower

Detached four-bay single-storey direct-entry thatched house, built c.1800. Entrance porch and two-bay extension to the north, c.1950. Oaten straw thatched roof hipped to the north and gabled to the south. Twisted ridge with bobbins and a central rendered chimneystack with a further rendered chimneystack rising from the south gable. Whitewashed clay walls with a setback to southern bay. Pebbledash render to rear. Two-over-two sash windows. Timber casement windows to rear. A single two-over-two iron swivel window to entrance porch. A former forge which retains many of its associated features. Positioned at a rural crossroads, this former forge is historically and socially important forming part of the social and economic structure of the locality.

Mountrice

Detached four-bay single-storey direct-entry thatched house, built c.1850, prolonged by various accretions and given a front entrance porch and gable-fronted shop unit added c.1940 to the side elevation. Oaten straw thatched roof, hipped to the north and gable-ended to the south. Having a twisted ridge with hazel scollops and bobbins to either end. Two rendered chimneystacks with capstones and terracotta pots. In the process of being re-thatched by Jack O'Donoghue. Painted rough-cast rendered walls. Located at important crossroads with wall-mounted post box and grotto. Much enhanced by the 1940s shopfront. Important example of crossroads house with a public use.

Mountrice

Seven-bay single-storey thatched lobby entry house, built c.1800, facing southwest. Single-bay thatched outbuilding to front. Three eastern bays and westernmost bay nineteenth century accretions. Oaten straw thatch roof hipped to east and gabled to west with concrete ridge. Twisted ridge and hazel scollops. Two brick chimneystacks, with dogtooth stringcourse. Whitewashed rough cast rendered walls, 500mm deep. Four-over-two and six-over-three timber sash windows. Tongued-and-grooved timber door to front porch. Open hearth with spy window to jamb wall survives intact. Early shutter boxes survive throughout with flat panelled shutters. Two-bay outbuilding, with the ridge of the hipped oaten thatch roof perpendicular to the house is located on the front site.

Quinsborough

Detached four-bay single-storey direct-entry thatched house, built c.1780, with a windbreaker entrance. Hipped oaten straw thatched roof with exposed scollops due to the poor state of the thatch. Centrally located rendered chimneystack. Whitewashed rough-cast rendered clay walls with rubble stone gables. Heavily battered north gable with buttress extending. Square-headed window openings with concrete sills and uPVC windows. Square-headed door opening set within the windbreaker having a flat-panelled timber door. Set parallel to the road enclosed by cement rendered walls forming a small front yard.

Quinsborough

Detached three-bay single-storey direct-entry thatched house, built c.1850, adjacent to the 24th Canal Lock, with a modern extension to the rear c.1990. Gabled pitched oaten straw thatched roof over galvanised metal, with a twisted ridge and interspersed bobbins. Centrally located brick chimneystack. Whitewashed over rubblestone walls approximately 600mm deep. Two-over-two timber sash windows. Square-headed door opening with a timber plank half-door c.1990. Open hearth visible to interior with rough timber lintel. Large extension to rear.

Toghereen

Detached five-bay single-storey direct-entry thatched house, built c.1840, with a windbreaker entrance. Hipped oaten straw thatched roof with plastic conduit scollops and a pair of rendered chimneystacks. Thatch in poor condition. Painted rough-cast render over rubblestone walls of 65cm in depth. Single-pane timber sash windows. Door opening set within windbreaker with a corrugated iron roof. Plank timber door and bottom leaf half-door. Site enclosed by rough-cast rendered walls with vehicular gate and pedestrian gate. Rubblestone outbuildings to west form a front yard.

Ballykelly

Detached six-bay single-storey direct-entry thatched house, built c.1800, with a two-bay lean-to slated return and a range of outbuildings to the rear. Gabled oaten straw thatched roof with twisted ridge. Three brick chimneystacks. Rough-cast rendered stone and clay walls. Boarded-up window openings except one having a two-over-two sash window and a wrought-iron grille. Square-headed door opening of late Victorian character having a glazed flat-panelled timber door with notched detailing and chrome Art Deco door furniture, flanked by glazed sidelights. Set perpendicular to the road enclosed by a ruled-and-lined rendered wall with square-plan piers and wrought-iron gates. Substantial stone outbuildings to the rear form a courtyard, all of which were formerly slated.

Oldgrange

Detached four-bay single-storey direct-entry thatched house, built c.1850. Gabled oaten straw thatched roof with a twisted ridge and hazel scollops to ridge and eaves. Two rendered chimneystacks, one to centre and gable. Painted pebbledash rendered rubble stone walls. Replacement timber casement windows and concrete sills. Square-headed door opening with a replacement timber panelled and glazed door. Set perpendicular to the road at a lower level with a concrete wall enclosing a tarmacadamed front side and rear site. Kept in excellent condition with much pride by owners. A modern family bungalow is located to the rear.

Coole

Detached four-bay single-storey thatched house, built c.1800, facing east, much enlarged to obscure original form by extensions to front and to rear. Hipped oaten thatched roof erected 2004, with a heat-treated log roof to the rear extension. Twisted ridge with hazel scollops to ridge and eaves. Pair of polychrome brick chimneystacks with clay pots. Cast-iron rainwater goods. Pebble dash rendered rubble stone walls. Four-pane timber casement windows, and modern timber sash windows. Fine site providing a wonderful setting for the house which is in very good repair.

Silot

Detached four-bay single-storey lobby-entry thatched house, built c.1800. Set perpendicular to the road with a front and rear yard. Hipped and gabled oaten thatch roof, erected c.1991 by Jack Donoghue, with a twisted ridge and a pair of brick chimneystacks. Pebble dash and rough cast rendered clay walls approximately 80 cm deep. Two-over-two timber sash windows, arranged in fashion similar to site 47 suggesting local building tradition. Plank timber door. Intact interior retaining tongued-and-grooved timber ceilings, plank timber doors and open hearth with spy window to lobby jamb wall. Added historical value attributed to its original form and many important external and internal features.

The Curragh

Detached four-bay single-storey thatched house, built c.1850, with a front entrance porch and a three-bay slated single-storey return, perpendicular to the road facing west. Hipped thatched roof with a sedge ridge detail, a half dormer to the south gable. Covered with chicken wire. Two pebble dash rendered chimneystacks. Natural slate roof to return formerly covered in corrugated-iron. Painted pebbledash rendered walls of approximately 3.5 feet in depth. uPVC windows. Modern timber panelled door to entrance porch and a plank timber half-door to the side entrance. The last remaining thatched house in the Curragh, this structure is of considerable value to the architectural variety of the region.

Cornalway, Kilcullen

Detached three-bay to front five-bay to side, single-storey thatched "gentleman's residence", c.1800, facing west with a front porch and a range of stone outbuildings to the north arranged around a farm yard. Sited within landscaped grounds with avenue entered through decorative cast-iron gates; enclosed by rubble stone walls; with mature beech trees. Hipped oaten thatch roof to the front pitch and south side. Corrugated sheeting to the inner pitches. Natural slate to the north wing. Thatched 2003 with a platted ridge and four large rendered chimneystacks; octagonal clay pots. Formally proportioned window openings with original sashes. Replacement timber door with rectangular overlight. To the rear of the south wing is a plank timber door opening into a small courtyard.

Gurteenuna

Detached four-bay single-storey lobby-entry thatched house, built c.1800, with a modern extension to rear, c.1990. Hipped oaten thatch roof with twisted and scolloped ridge. Brick chimneystack. Whitewashed lime rendered walls approximately 65cm in thickness. uPVC windows and replacement double-leaf timber door c.1990. Set perpendicular to the road accessed by a short drive with a large landscaped site to the side. While the renovation of this house has led to the loss of its windows and doors it remains a good example of a thatched house occupied by a young family, with a relatively discreet extension to the rear.

Clonegath

Detached four-bay single-storey thatched house, built c.1780, facing west, much enlarged by two two-storey extensions including a return and an L-plan two-storey block to rear, built c.1975. Hipped reed thatched roof to all sections with decorative boxed raised ridges and with hazel scollops, with half dormers to rear. Rendered clay walls to original house. Multi-pane timber casement windows and concrete sills; one six-over-three timber sash window. Once an average-sized thatched dwelling extensively extended on an L-plan over two storeys. Although there appear to be few original features left the highly visible location gives this site added significance.

Cloncarlin

Detached four-bay single-storey thatched house, built c.1900, enlarged by accretions one forming an attached single-bay thatched-roofed section with lower ridge to the west and a slated section to the east. Pitched oaten straw thatched roof in a very poor state of repair, with a pair of cement block rendered chimneystacks. Pebbledash rendered clay walls. Square-headed window openings, enlarged horizontally, with timber casement windows. Square-headed door opening with a hardwood timber panelled door. This house is in a poor state of repair and while there are few original features evident the house embodies the traditional approach to enlarging a small three-bay thatched house.

Kileen West, Riverstown Crossroads	Kileen West	Harristown Upper	Walterstown	Nurney	Blackditch

Kileen West, Riverstown Crossroads

Detached four-bay single-storey thatched clay-built house, built c.1800, with a derelict outbuilding to the rear. Hipped oaten thatch roof with twisted ridge and rows of scollops to ridge and eaves. . Rebuilt redbrick chimneystack with terracotta pot. Whitewash over clay walls of approximately 75cm thick. Square-headed window openings to front elevation only, with six-over-three timber sash windows c.1850, having splayed reveals and cement sills. Square-headed door opening with replacement timber plank half-door c.1995, opening onto a limestone flag. Set perpendicular and back from the road with access via a lane shared with a neighbouring thatched house. One of the most intact houses in the county enhanced by its proximity to No.63, separated by a raised meadow, forming a picturesque rural setting.

Kileen West

Detached three-bay single-storey thatched house, built c.1800, on L-plan with single-bay gabled addition, c.1900, prolonged by a tin-roof outbuilding. Hipped oaten thatch roof, gabled to the front projection with rough timber frame and a roped scolloped ridge and scolloped eaves. Central rendered chimneystack; another brick chimneystack to gable having an angled stringcourse. Painted rough-cast render over clay and stone walls of c.70cm in depth. Two-over-two timber sash windows, set in exposed sash boxes; cement sills; casement window to accretion. Cylinder glass throughout. Tongued-and-grooved timber door to shallow wind breaker. Facing south perpendicular to lane with front site enclosed by rendered wall; wrought-iron gates. Enhanced by its proximity to No.62, separated by a raised meadow, forming a picturesque rural setting.

Harristown Upper

Detached four-bay single-storey former thatched house, built c.1850, now with a corrugated iron roof and obscured by growth. Hipped corrugated iron roof. The site is overgrown with vegetation and not accessible.

Walterstown

Detached six-bay single-storey L-plan lobby-entry thatched house, built c.1820, facing east with later accretions including entrance porch, and outbuilding to south, possibly built as a byre. Outbuilding to front site, enclosed by low wall from road. Hipped oaten thatch roof with a plaited ridge and two rows of scollops. Two brick chimneystacks with terracotta pots. Thatched corrugated iron porch roof. Rough cast rendered clay walls c.80 cm deep. Rubble stone and brick walls to rear with some concrete. Two-over-two timber sash windows and exposed sash boxes. One three-over-three sash and timber casement windows to rear. Square-headed door opening with replacement timber panelled door. Tongued-and-grooved panelling to lobby and kitchen ceilings. Original open hearth with range and oak trunk lintel.

Nurney

Detached five-bay single-storey lobby-entry thatched house, built c.1800. Set back from road down a lane with a cobbled yard to the east enclosed by stone and concrete outbuildings. Oaten thatch hipped roof with plaited scalloped ridge. A central rebuilt brick chimneystack with a further brick chimneystack rising from either end with a square profile clay pot. Rough-cast rendered clay walls 90 cm deep. Stone wheel guard to corner. Door opening with hardwood panelled door. Two-over-two timber windows. Windows to rear appear much earlier in date with two-over-two and six-over-one sashes, all c.1800. Intact interior with three roomed plan extended by room to east possibly a converted byre. Open hearth with wrought-iron furniture, oven, spy window and open chimney flu.

Blackditch

Detached four-bay single-storey lobby-entry thatched house, built c.1945, with extension to rear, c.1990. Oaten thatch to front pitch only with a plaited ridge. Corrugated sheet iron to rear pitch (with thatch intact beneath). Two red brick chimneystacks to gables. Pan tiled roof to extension. Pebble dash rendered mass concrete walls. Square-headed window openings with three-over-six timber sashes and metal casement to central bay. Original tongued-and-grooved timber half door with iron hinges and a modern hardwood glazed timber door. A traditional layout of small lobby and three rooms, retaining its tongued-and-grooved timber ceiling, open hearth with spy window and iron hearth furniture, plank timber doors and panelling. Home to son of the thatcher Pat Molloy.

Balls Hill

Detached four-bay single-storey direct-entry former thatched house, built c.1800, with a windbreaker entrance. Hipped corrugated iron roof, with a central rendered chimneystack and a brick stack rising from the west side elevation. Painted rough-cast rendered clay walls with smooth render plinth course. Square-headed window openings with timber casement windows and concrete sills. Square-headed timber panelled door set within a windbreaker. Site enclosed from road by rubblestone wall incorporating outbuilding with corrugated tin roof structure. Steel gates hang from cast concrete piers with stop-chamfered edges. Although the roof has been covered with corrugated iron, the rest of the house seems to have been retained.

Calverstown

Detached five-bay single-storey former lobby-entry thatched house, built c.1850, enlarged to incorporate later historic accretions including porch and return. Extensively renovated and modernised c.2004. Reed thatch roof, gabled to the west side and to the return, hipped to the east side. Raised scolloped ridge and eaves, erected c.2004. Pair of rebuilt brick chimneystacks, to centre and to gable. Cement coping to the gable elevation. Painted rough-cast rendered rubblestone walls with a buttress to the front elevation. Square-headed window openings with replacement one-over-one timber sash windows and concrete sills. Flat-roofed square-plan porch with replacement timber glazed door. Further porch to rear with modern tongued-and-grooved timber door. Set parallel to the road enclosed by rendered walls with tin roofed outbuilding.

Greatrath

Detached four-bay two-storey gable-ended thatched house, built before 1710, prolonged by slate-roofed single-storey extension to south, c.1900. Two-storey return to rear. Accessed by lane with site enclosed by wrought-iron agricultural fencing. Farm yard to east with stone outbuildings. Rope ridged pitched oaten thatch roof. Brick chimneystacks rise from gables. Roof structure replaced c.1900 and elevation lowered. Roughcast rendered clay walls, c.90 cm deep. Rubble stone walls to the rear. Intact interior ceiling panelling, nineteenth century doors and panelled window linings. Large open hearth with remains of stone oven built into the rear wall of the house. The front door opens into an entrance hall with terrazzo flooring. Timber staircase inserted c.1900, with half landing to the return.

Kilrush, Athy

Detached three-bay two-storey thatched house, built c.1730, facing north. Front entrance porch, flat-roof section to rear and lean-to to east all form later extensions. Set back from the road accessed by a long lane with front lawn enclosed by wrought-iron railing and a farm yard to the east with stone outbuildings. Hipped oaten thatched roof with a plaited ridge. One central brick chimneystack with clay pots. Corrugated iron roof covering to lean-to and return. Rendered clay walls, rough cast to rear. Square-headed window openings with uPVC windows and painted granite sills throughout. Replacement hardwood glazed door and sidelights. Intact interior with tongued-and-grooved timber panelling and terracotta tiled floors. Open hearth arch now accommodating a solid fuel range.

Fontstown

Detached four-bay single-storey former direct-entry thatched house, built c.1800, with a front entrance porch and porch to rear. Hipped oaten straw thatched roof with a twisted ridge and bobbins. Bamboo scollops to ridge and eaves. Rendered chimneystack. Whitewashed rough-cast rendered rubblestone walls, c.80cm deep. Large buttress to rear elevation. One-over-one timber sash windows and concrete sills. Early four-pane timber casement window to rear. Modern timber glazed panelled door to the front entrance porch, added c.1970, with timber casement windows to the sides. Facing south on a corner site at the Fontstown crossroads. Enclosed by a low rendered wall with coping. Front gravelled yard area enclosed to west by a rubblestone outbuilding.

Ballynabarna

Detached four-bay single-storey lobby-entry thatched house, built c.1800, with windbreaker and single-storey addition to rear, c.1950. Hipped oaten straw thatched roof, sheet metal to rear, with twisted scolloped ridge and scolloped eaves. Brick chimneystack with clay pots. Whitewashed rough-cast render rubble limestone walls. Windows enlarged with concrete sills and timber casement windows. Square-headed door opening to windbreaker entrance having a replacement hardwood glazed panelled door. Set parallel to the road with a large landscaped front site enclosed by rendered walls. Lofted two-bay stone outbuilding to the south with gauged brick carriage arches. Wrought-iron gates give access to the gravelled drive with a further decorative 'horsegate' to the front garden. A modern farmyard is located to the north.

Ballynagussan	Kilcon	Castlereban North	Castlereban North	Ballyroe	Tullygorey

Ballynagussan

Detached four-bay single-storey direct-entry thatched house, built c.1800, facing south with later entrance porch. Oaten straw thatched roof hipped to east, gabled to west. Plastic conduit scollops to ridge and wire scollops to eaves. Rendered chimneystack with a terracotta pot. Rendered clay walls of c.74cm deep. Tapered buttress to rear. Square-headed window openings with one-over-one sashes. Timber casement windows to rear. Interior thoroughly renovated c.1984 leaving very few internal original features. The three room layout remains. Situated along the road with gravelled front site and wrought-iron gate giving access to site. Separate structure positioned to west set closer to the road, which formerly housed a local shop run by the former owners of the house, the Conlon sisters.

Kilcon

Detached four-bay single-storey gabled direct-entry thatched house, built c.1800. Oaten straw thatched roof, hipped to the east, gabled to the west with hazel scollops ridge and to eaves. A central brick chimneystack with cement flashing to the stack and cement coping to the gable. Lime washed rubble stone walls to the front elevation, cement rendered to the gable and rough-cast render to the rear. Square-headed window openings to front elevation only, with one-over-one timber sash windows c.1940 and cement sills. Square-headed door opening to the eastern most bay with an original plank timber door. House is set perpendicular to the road facing north with a front gravelled yard enclosed by stone outbuildings and a rendered wall to the road.

Castlereban North

Detached four-bay single-storey direct-entry thatched house, built c.1850, with lean-to extension to rear, built c.1995. Hipped oaten straw thatched roof with twisted and scolloped ridge. Scolloped hip and eaves. Decorative bobbins interspersed along ridge. Rendered walls to front, with rough-cast rendered rubble stone walls to other elevations. Square-headed window openings, enlarged c.1980, with timber casement windows and concrete sills. Door opening to southernmost bay with replacement timber plank door. Tongued-and-grooved half door in front of full door leaf. Set with south gable facing bend in road enclosed by metal gates and a pair of modern stone and brick piers giving access to a front yard. Tin roof outbuildings attached to the north gable.

Castlereban North

Detached five-bay single-storey gable-ended thatched house, built c.1900, with a gabled entrance porch. Pitched oaten thatch roof with a twisted ridge and interspersed straw bobbins. Hazel scollops to the ridge and eaves. Centrally placed modern rendered chimneystack and cement coping to both gables. Painted pebbledash render brick walls. Square-headed window openings with uPVC windows and replacement composite granite sills. Replacement tongued-and-grooved timber half door to porch. Overlight to gable with vertical glazing bars. Set parallel to the road with narrow front site enclosed by a rendered brick and stone wall with wrought-iron gates. To the rear is a redbrick two-storey outbuilding.

Ballyroe

Detached three-bay single-storey thatched house, built c.1820, facing north with three-bay accretion to east c.1910. Current L-plan form created by a two-bay section added to the east c.1987. Oaten thatched roof, hipped to north, gabled to east. Twisted ridge with hazel scollops to ridge and eaves. Two rendered chimneystacks. Owner recalls natural timber A-framed roof with bark attached. Rough-cast rendered redbrick walls to original section, cement rendered elsewhere. Buttress to east elevation of main house. Replacement hardwood casement windows. Replacement half-door. Limestone step under open porch, supported by timber posts. Hearth rebuilt and layout reconfigured, c.1999. Original section set perpendicular to road. The brick walled construction is explained by location of a brick field across the road adjacent to canal.

Tullygorey

Detached three-bay single-storey thatched house, built c.1800, with a front entrance porch c.1950, and a lean-to section to the west side elevation. Hipped thatched roof now covered with polythene. Rendered chimneystack. Coursed rubble stone walls with lime mortar and squared limestone quoins to the corners. Square-headed window openings with timber casement windows. Replacement timber panelled door c.1980. Built parallel to the road facing south with no rear boundary evident. This is a very small modest house which is in a derelict condition. The significance of this structure lies in its use of limestone construction in an area of mostly clay walled houses.

Rosebran

Detached five-bay single-storey former thatched house, built c.1850, prolonged to one site by byre and a lean-to porch extension to opposite end. Coated corrugated metal covered gabled roof structure with cement coping to the gables and a single rendered chimneystack. Painted pebbledash rendered stone walls with a rendered plinth course. Square-headed window openings enlarged c.1980, with timber casement windows and concrete sills. Square-headed door opening to the lean-to with a timber panelled and glazed timber door. Hard surface front site. This former thatched house has been re-covered in modern sheet iron. Apart from this alteration the house appears to be intact.

Derryoughter West

Detached three-bay single-storey semi direct-entry thatched house, built c.1850, with a three-bay single-storey flat-roofed extension to the rear, built c.1975. Hipped oaten straw thatched roof with a twisted ridge and interspersed straw bobbins. Bamboo scollops to the ridge and eaves and a rebuilt red brick chimneystack with terracotta pots. Whitewashed roughcast render over mud walls of approximately 45cm in thickness. Battered gables. Square-headed window openings with timber casement windows c.1975 and concrete sills. Square-headed door opening with timber panelled door having an oval glazed panel and a plank timber half door (lower half only). An intact interior with an open hearth with solid fuel range inserted. Tongued-and-grooved ceiling panelling to both rooms.

Grangechiggin

Detached four-bay single-storey lobby-entry thatched house, built c.1800, facing south with a two-bay single-storey extension to east and a five-bay dormer single-storey extension perpendicular to west, c.2003. Complex hipped oaten straw thatched roof with a twisted ridge and bobbins. Bamboo scollops to the ridge and wire scollops to the eaves. The owner remembers some oak beams in the roof structure. A pair of chimneystacks to the original section and several dormers and half-dormers to the late section. Whitewash rendered clay walls. Square-headed window openings with replacement timber casement windows and stone sills. Square-headed door openings with replacement tongued-and-grooved timber doors to front and rear. Apart from an intact lobby the interior has been completely reconfigured and modernised in a vernacular style.

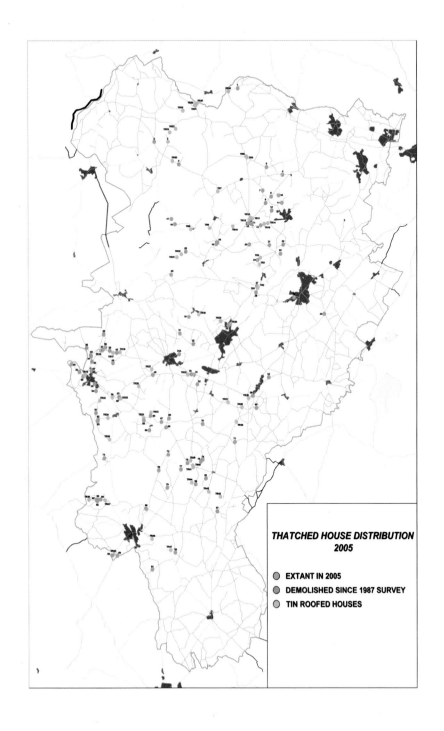

THATCHED HOUSE DISTRIBUTION
2005

● EXTANT IN 2005
● DEMOLISHED SINCE 1987 SURVEY
● TIN ROOFED HOUSES